A SOLDIER IN THE LORD'S ARMY

BY

JERRY ONYEKA

ISBN: **978-0-620-99408-8**

Published by

Jerry Onyeka

For more information or bulk request, contact:

pstjerryonyeka@gmail.com

+27633028341

Printed by

Minuteman Press Somerset West

ACKNOWLEDGEMENT

With appreciation to God almighty for the call into ministry and the help of the Holy Spirit my source of inspiration and teacher for guiding me throughout the writing of this book.

CONTENTS

INTRODUCTION

Thou art my battle axe and weapons of war, for with thee I will break in pieces the nations and with thee will I destroy kingdoms.

Jeremiah 51:20

CHAPTER ONE

The Life Of A Soldier

I recently watched a military recruitment training, it is a training designed to rewire your thinking and your subconscious mind. The military commander aim is to flush away everything you have grown to know as normal in order to create a new normal and norm into you. The training changes your life, right from going to bed and when you wake up, to when you eat and how you eat. You are given a specific minute to finish an assignment, failure to do your assignment at a particular allotted time you will be disciplined for it. I heard the commander telling the new soldiers the only language that is allowed in the military is just two words, anything more than those two words gets you in trouble. The words are; **'YES SIR'**. With my civilian eyes and way of judgment I called the whole thing unfair and unjust treatment. You are tempted to want to challenge the commander. Imagine having a lot to say and not be allowed to say it. Imagined seeing things that seems wrong and not have the audacity to address it. They have a code that must not be violated, if you are found wanting in any of the code you may be court marshalled or dismissed from the military. The military strips you of yourself to create a new self within you. The new self is not the one your parents raised, the idea is that they must be the one that determine the character and thoughts that goes through and out of your mind. They will never give you a responsibility without adequately training and trusting you to be able to handle it. They train you to always defend the interest of your commander. A true soldier knows what his commander would do in any situation. The military owns your thoughts and imagination. No matter how good you think your intentions are, you are not permitted to go through with it without getting clearance. You dare not murmur no matter how unpleasant the order is. The military will make sure during the course of the training that nothing could come from you that is not subject to the commander's order. A soldier does not belong to themselves and will never do anything that does not benefit the military interest. You are a soldier to serve the interest of the boss not yours. In fact, *a soldier is dead to self and alive only to service.* No matter how dangerous a place is, when you are commanded to go there, you must say **'YES SIR'**. You don't argue, you can't do or say otherwise. Soldiers are trained never to fear. In the training ground every fear you came with will be destroyed, the commander will make sure of it. When you are commanded to look ahead then ahead you must look, even if your mother that you have not seen for years or months stands by your side. You dare not turn to greet her or you would be penalized. *Life of a soldier is a life of service and selflessness.* No matter how smart or rich you are, you must be subject to the captain's command. If it is the military you want to join, then your family background has nothing to do with the kind of training you would receive. There is no special treatment in the military, everyone under goes the same training and discipline.

The reason why the people in our team (ministry) behave the way they do today, is because the character in them was not planted by the leadership of the team. We treat people with so much caution so we don't lose them. We allow certain obnoxiousness to thrive in our team because we are too afraid to address the nonsense of people. Why hire people you can't fire?

The moment people think they are indispensable is the very moment their stay in expires. The reason why people think they are indispensable is because the leader treats them that way. And as they continue to think that way, they will not see the need to work hard or try to develop further. They begin to decline in growth unconsciously. It is very dangerous to get there in life, and if you mistakenly see yourself in that position where something tells you, you are now indispensable, for your own good run to someone at the junior level of your career and intentionally ask him or her to refresh your memories on things you already know. Whenever a teacher becomes a student pride dies, he learns, he becomes a better teacher. *But if a teacher decides to stay in his teacher's euphoria, he will soon become outdated and even his students will become his boss soon enough.* So, if we must do better than we did yesterday we must learn better than we did a day before. Advancement in knowledge is advancement in career. Those who refuse to learn will remain in their yesterday while those who learns will always own the future. For tomorrow belong to those who sees every opportunity to do better and grabs it. Every system has a code and it is called code of conduct. A true soldier does not respond with violence in every altercation, the code must be followed. You are not permitted to bring shame to the military body and you are not expected to fight with a civilian and lose. So, you are reminded to be selective in things you get yourself involved with. You must fight every battle with a constant consciousness of your commander's demand, your actions must bring glory to the unit and the captain, failure to do so would attract certain penalties. A real soldier is not defined by uniform, anybody can actually get the uniform from a clothing store, neither are they defined by words, rather it is action that defines a true soldier. A soldier has a refined military character that is infused in them by the commander through training. There is no room for questionable character. You are not permitted to carry a character that was not planted in you by the captain. That was why Jesus spent three years training his disciples before he would send them. Those who would succeed him in continuing the spreading of the gospel after he has gone back to the father. He made sure they were adequately trained and well informed on how to carry on without him, making sure the gospel does not die with him when he dies. The reason a vision dies once the visionary dies is because the issue of training was not prioritized. What training does is, it transfers the entire knowledge of the trainer into the trainee. Sometimes the training can be very intense that the trainee mistakes his teacher's intentions for wickedness. Every teacher has their own traditionally adopted patterns of transferring knowledge, a wise student would follow the steps of his teacher instead of challenging it. Any student that challenges the method of his teacher will receive little or no education from his teacher. Jesus taught his disciples, that the way to overcome hate was through love, and the way to overcome evil was to be good. You don't overcome a thing by becoming it you overcome it by choosing to be different from others. He made sure he taught them the method of the kingdom and immediately he was certain they got it he said my time is at hand. When knowledge is not transferred people suffer the consequences of ignorance and ignorance is costly. Every generation must have a willing teacher and willing students, men who are willing to learn despite the cost required. If it cost what it cost the wise will pay what has to be paid. I have seen student cry and return back to school the next day to continue in what made them cry the previous day because they were certain that where they want to get to in life requires that they passed through that road. Yet I have seen students who walked off for whatever reasons from the class room and never returned ever again. The thing is the one who retuned back to school becomes what he was studying to become but the one who did not return never became what he had wanted to become. Why? You can't become something if you don't accept the discipline and the training it requires.

CHAPTER TWO

T he bible calls us soldiers in the Lord's army and we all know that we are military by training and recruitment not just by uniform and by words. Though in the military there are dress codes, but it does not mean that anyone that puts on that dress automatically becomes a soldier. I know in today's altar call, it is not thoroughly explained to the new converts or intended converts that what they are getting into is an intense military training. Where everything that gives you confidence will be taken away from you, your family background consciousness will die, your academic prowess consciousness will surrender, and your beauty consciousness will be submitted. Pride will be knocked off your life. You will undergo this intense training till anything that you derive pride and confidence in will be totally wiped off your life. The goal here is not to render you useless but that nothing else gets the glory in your life but God and God alone, nothing else. Our God is a jealous God, who though loves his children to have the best of everything but anything that gets more attention in your life than him will be taken away from you. He clearly declared, *"I will never share my glory with anyone"* is a non-negotiable decree. Soldiers will never hand you a uniform till you have been trained adequately, but there is a uniform for rookies in the military. If you are a person that understands the military code, once you see trainees you will know. Likewise, they won't hand you a weapon till you have been trained on both how to use the weapon and how to avoid getting killed in the battlefield. *The reason why many Christian today are fallen from grace and fallen in battles is because some Christians lack adequate training.* The reason being that, some people did not know what Christianity is all about. Some also are unnecessarily busy for the new recruits. In the military there are people responsible for training new recruits most times. They are not all about going out there and fighting. They specialize in training and equipping those who will go into the warzone and fight for the glory of the nation. But if everybody wants to see the war front nobody will train the warriors and lack of training will spell danger to the entire unit. The body of Christ is in a certain state because of lack of proper orientation, proper military orientation is pivotal in today's Christianity.

In Jesus training ground the disciples were told the danger that awaits them if they decide to follow him. Jesus never showed them nice shoes, nice houses, nice cars and jet. No, they were never shown anything material. They were shown a cross and tribulation. "**Mathew 16:24**, *then Jesus said to his disciples, whoever wants to be my disciple must deny themselves and take up their cross and follow me*". It was clear to the disciples what they were getting into and by Jesus' teachings he had acquired big enemies for himself. Political and religious leaders hated him and wanted him dead. His enemies were the high and mighty of their days which had the power to kill anyone they seem not to like their face or anyone that introduces another law or teachings that contradicts their traditional practices. In fact following Jesus carried all kinds of danger for his disciples. Yet they followed him wherever he went. **"Then Thomas said to his fellow disciples, let us also go that we may die with him"**. These were men who understood what they were doing. Because their captain took time to train them to understand what his message is about and the danger and the opposition that will meet them. It is true that there is blessing in the body of Christ and it is also true that it is not always fun being a Christian. We are in the world where truth is considered a hate speech. It was almost the same in the days of the apostles, Paul in his writings made it clear that *'nothing can be done against the truth but for the truth'.* Training enlarges our capacity and enables us to have balance in the affairs of life. The scripture is full of stories of people of God facing all kinds of tribulation yet in our today's Christianity those stories are almost silent and the areas that declares blessings are made national anthem in our churches. So, if a Christian faces an opposition, he /she wouldn't know what to do or how to stand. You will see them running from one place to the other seeking for solution. Training is very important, without it many will rise and fall back down. There are many falls that should have been avoided if men were trained. Where would pride come from? Pride is a product of self-consciousness, in order to avoid pride self must die. Once pride dies assignment becomes the reason for living, and your value will be tied to productivity. Also, in the body of Christ, we are rated according to kingdom fruitfulness.

Be Purpose Driven

Being purpose driven and not money driven will get you to your desired dreams and aspiration. Money is good but money is a distractor. If money is what drives you, you can easily give up on your dreams and go for a money-making scheme. Once you begin to make money it has the capacity of blinding you from your purpose. Money opens our eyes to material things and blinds our eyes from eternal things. Everything gotten with money on earth will be left behind but everything gotten from following your God given purpose will follow you to eternity. *Pursuing purpose attracts money but following money most times distracts from purpose.* There are people who would have become great doctors, great lawyers, great accountant, great pastors and pilots and some many other things who didn't become because they were lured out of their purpose by the color of little money and flashy clothes and pleasure. Meanwhile all the things the devil uses to distract one from his purpose could actually become his after purpose has been actualized. Satan never shows you anything that is not in your destiny. Anything he tries to use today to draw you to himself away from God is in your tomorrow, if you can be patience and wait a little while you will see much more than that in your hands. Mammon has drawn many away from their duty post for God, actually, some preacher no longer preaches Christ. If our prosperity is only in mundane things, we have ourselves become failures in the kingdom of God. God wants us to have earthly riches, Yes He wants us to enjoy the best things of this world but not at the expense of our soul, not at the expense of our calling, and not at the expense of our assignment. When money increases and our spiritual life declines, we must run to God and ask him to strengthen our spiritual life and give us balance prosperity that does not leave our soul behind. Those who believe money is everything will do whatever and anything to have it even when it means losing their soul in the process. **Oswald J Smith** pleaded with the Lord; "*I have only one life to live I want to invest it for thee*". As he continues to pledge in prayer, asking God to use him; *"make me a soul winner, send me out as an evangelist. Let me see revival. Let me live for other. Let blessing rest upon my ministry"*. He asked questions too; *"What are the qualifications? How may I be used, are there conditions? If so, reveal them to me"* this were his cry day and night. If anyone tells you there are no conditions to being used, sorry you have been lied to. God allows everyone to come to him but does not use just everyone to reveal himself. Selflessness is a cure for selfishness. If anything, God cannot use a selfish person. You must be selfless to see things the way God sees them and to reach those He is trying to reach. A selfish person cannot go to places that endangers him in anyway even when God requires it from him. Paul was not only willing to be jailed for the gospel's sake but to die too. That is why in GOD'S training camp He takes us through different kinds of training in order to rid us of things that could pose as hinderance to the fulfilling of our divine assignment. Any ideas, thoughts and hunger that cannot be found in GOD must be removed from us, if it is Him, we wish to represent. Are you willing to enlist into the lord's army? Then let the things of this world matter less to you and let the things of eternity take the chief place in your heart.

Mathew 6:30-33;
Now if God so clothes the grass of the field, which today is, and tomorrow is thrown into the oven, will He not much more clothe you, O you of little faith? Therefore, do not worry, saying, 'What shall we eat?' or 'What shall we drink?' or 'What shall we wear?' For after all these things the Gentiles seek. For your heavenly Father knows that you need all these things. But seek first the kingdom of God and His righteousness, and all these things shall be added to you.

CHAPTER THREE

The Inevitable
Of A Soldier

A soldier story cannot be complete without a testimony of hardship suffered in the course of service. Hardship experience is part of every soldier's story. There is no way your faithfulness to God can be proven without a visible and invincible hardship. Life of a soldier is full of messy situation but what makes a true soldier is his ability to match on inspite of the many trials and tribulations that he may encounter on his way of assignment. A sign up to military is a sign up to die. And death is the destiny of every man, one thing no human can postponed or delay is the day of his death. What then matters is how and where a person died. It matters to your commander how a soldier died. If he dies in battle, he will receive a state or national burial and will be tagged a hero but if he dies in a place that has no connection to his assignment and duty he will be buried as an ordinary citizen. Though we are all afraid to die yet our glory will be determined only by death.

Paul in charging his son Timothy told him the realities of a soldier and how he must stand to be able to face everything that lingers up against him in his evangelical trips.

"2 Timothy 2:3 you therefore must endure hardship as a good soldier of Jesus Christ". When men are not intentionally discipled guesswork becomes mentorship programs, thoughts becomes mentors, and careless dreams becomes a charge to kill our loved ones. Hardship is something that you will endure as a soldier, you can't run from it. Even your message might not be accepted

at your first preaching. You therefore must be consistent in season and out of season till somebody pays attention to you. The truth is, in our world today there are many speakers. The social media is speaking, sickness and diseases are speaking, the devil is speaking, false teachers are also speaking and there are voices in our heads too that sometimes sounds like the nicest thing ever but are contrary to the ways and word of God. Therefore, you must intentionally introduce and keep speaking the word of God till the world understands what you are trying to communicate. *Only those who have been taught the power of consistency can withstand the frustration of being ignored, and never gives up.* Apostle Paul made his struggles as a preacher known to every believer, he never hid it from them, and he made sure they understood the blessings of being afflicted for Christ's sake. Anything suffered in the name of Jesus carries with it a mighty reward. So, in their days whatever they suffer is publicly shared as a testimony, rather than being discouraged tribulations actually encouraged them. They count it a worthy gift to suffer for the gospel's sake. I am not in any ways trying to endorse suffering, but as a soldier we know that the only way to promotion is battles and challenges faced. Nobody laughs his way to the top, nobody celebrates his ways to victory, and victory is not gotten by clapping of hands but by the throwing of punches. In the world of immorality and all kinds of evil rights being claimed by different society, it is becoming difficulty by the day to stand upright in the world today but **God said that those who endures to the end shall be saved.**

CHAPTER FOUR

PERSECUTION

"Yea, and all that will live godly in Christ Jesus will be persecuted. 2Timothy 3:12"

Persecution means hostility, ill treatment and everything that is wrong. In some place just preaching the gospel is considered a crime. It is a crime to talk to your neighbors about the Lord, but as a soldier in Christ you must understand that a call to preach is a call to war against the kingdom of darkness and many world leaders are the agent of darkness. You ask 'what do you mean? Check their laws and things they stand for almost all of them is what God and His word is against. How can we allow our children to be deceived so heavily by the devil, we are in the world where we allow the world system to mentor our children for us. The social media takes the lead in many family's settings. Where our youth don't know any biblical character but almost all the immoral celebrities of the world are known by our children. Most people are afraid to speak because of persecution but the word of God has already told us aforetime that those that will live and stand for the advancement of Godly life in Christ must face persecution. We must learn to braze ourselves as soldiers in the lord's army and fight. There is a better and worst place than this world. If you stand for righteousness the better place will be yours to inherit but if you cowardly decide to join the world immoral system the worst place becomes your inheritance. Imagine what is happening today, sin is promoted on every platform, wherever you turn there is something that defiles the spirit, there are all kind of immoral indorsement wherever you turn on social media and in the world. No wonder the psalmist screamed *"let the words of my mouth and the meditation of my heart be acceptable in your sight oh lord my strength and my redeemer"*. We need an intentional commitment to praying for our thoughts and mouth. There are all kinds of things the devil fires on these areas of our body that we must engage in fire prayer for the protection of this areas of our lives. A Christian life is that of constant warfare. If there is no battle in your life currently you must provoke one. *Because as long as your presence is useful to the kingdom of God the kingdom of darkness will rise against you.* Anytime you see the armies of darkness in uproar against you, you are causing a very critical commotion in their kingdom. Most Christian when they face diverse tribulation, they think they have failed not knowing that is when they are winning. God cannot promote you without a battle. He must give you a mountain to take down. Every time God wants to deal with any situation on earth, He uses a man to accomplish it. Persecution is part of the blessing. Matured men in this kingdom matter sees tribulation as a blessing but children see it as a problem. A man of God always prays that God sends him affliction because he feasts on them to the shame of the devil. Nobody in Christ who is truly in Christ that is walking this sinful world will escape persecution. It will rise against you but certainly you will rise above it in victory.

CHAPTER FIVE

Sheep Among
Wolves

As long as you are a Christian in this world the world will never like you. Altar calls sounds amazing but the truth about it is immediately you walk out of that place you have made yourself a target. Some people's business and families begins to fall apart immediately they decide to accept the Lord and oftentimes people misunderstand this and starts to draw back and wonder if they made a huge mistake of accepting the Lord into their lives. The truth of the matter is, you made no mistake, infact you made the best decision of accepting the Lord. What happened is those in Christ is the enemy of the devil and he would do anything within his power to drag you back to himself. It's like working for a boss whose sexual advances you rejects. Such boss will make your life a living hell. If they can't sack you they will make things uncomfortable for you till you give in to their demands or get fired. Anybody who is in Christ is an automatic enemy to the devil and he will use his agents to fight you. The devil has his agents everywhere including inside the church so, as a child of God who has signed up into the Lord's army you must braze up yourself and get ready for whatever the devil throws at you. Jesus told his disciples in *Mathew 10:16, behold, I send you forth as sheep in the midst of wolves; be ye therefore wise as serpents, and harmless as doves.* A serpent is always ready to strike when an enemy comes up against him yet he is never distracted from his target. Every soldier must understand when a false alarm is made in order to throw him off balance and when an alarm that must get his attention should.

The devil uses all kinds of weapon against the children of God and among his most effective weapon is distractions. Many people lose their auxiliary because of distraction, I have seen somebody running at the highest speed in a running competition looks away from the line due to distraction and falls back in pace and loses the race. The devil is in the business of finding a believer's weakness and once he finds it, he strikes with every arsenal in his disposal. That is why the bible highly recommends that we die to flesh. We must die daily like Apostle Paul declared in, **1Corinthians 15:31 "I protest by your rejoicing which I have in Christ Jesus our lord, I die daily".** We must intentionally attack the flesh in the place of prayer whenever he wants to cooperate with the devil against the spirit.

In a battlefield a wise soldier never sleeps with his both eyes closed. You must be awake in spirit if you must win this battle. The more you defeat the devil the more he recruits more agent against you. So, to be on the safe side you must constantly arm yourself in case of sudden uproars. Sometimes you overcome a particular addiction or urge, the feeling leaves you and you never have them again. But, one month, five months, a year or two passes the same feelings resurfaces again and you wonder where it came from. I thought I had overcome this, you ask? Yes, you did overcame but the devil came back to see if he can get you to fall into it again. Look no one is totally free from temptation as long as you are still walking the face of the earth.

Mathew 12:43-45, when the unclean spirit is gone out of a man, he walketh through dry places, seeking rest, and findeth none. Then he saith I will return into my house from whence I came out and when he is come, he findeth it empty, swept and garnished. Then goeth he, and taketh with himself seven other spirit more wicked than himself and they enter in and dwell there; and the last state of that man is worse than the first even so shall it be also unto this wicked generation.

The devil is always coming back hoping to find you off-guard in order to destroy you. What he doesn't want to see is you accomplishing your divine purpose on earth. He knows the reward that awaits every soldier that finishes well in spite of all the fiery darts of the enemy that is thrown at him. The early Christians in Romans Empire were thrown to the lions and people used to stand and watch it as we watch soccer and other games today. Other times they were used as streets lights to light up the streets of Rome at nights. Yet the more persecution they faced the stronger their faith and the more people were converted. *In the face of death they were busy accepting the Lord.* Accepting the Lord back then was seen as dead sentence yet people trooped in to Christianity. They so loved the Lord that they were willing to die for the gospel. My question is, what kind of doctrine were they taught? What kind of discipleship did they go through? If the gospel was committed into your hands back then would this generation still have the gospel today? What we have today are people who will reject Christ immediately they go hungry for a day, some will turn to the devil if their churches are not growing as they had expected. Some so-called pastors and so-called prophets have been caught with fetish items in the name of trying to grow their churches and they have all kinds of reasons to justify their actions which among those reasons are persecution and suffering. When people are not adequately discipled, they will easily fall into the trap of the devil and as they fall in, they are bound to take many along with them. Beware not to fall into the hands of *"result is the sign of God's approval in a man's life";* That is a total lie, not every result is of God and whenever you find yourself in an environment where all you are pointed to is results and not Christ, you are in a wrong environment and must do everything possible to get out of such place. Whenever your heart is burgled with the urge to grow your bank account instead of growing the territorial control of GOD kingdom on earth you must go back to the drawing board to know the reason why Christ died. We are in a warzone and be careful not to be recruited by the soldiers of darkness. Because if earthly possession becomes your only motivation, you are on your way to hell. Turn back from where you are fallen and readjust your mindset and turn to the Lord and submit yourself to His will being done on earth as it is in heaven.

CHAPTER SIX

Christianity Is A
Warfront

"This is war, and there is no neutral ground. If you are not on my side, you're the enemy; if you're not helping, you're making things worse; Luke 11:23"

T here is no neutral position in this world, is either you are on the Lord side or you are on the devil side. Nobody is useless everybody is being used by something. If you are not being used by God you are being used by the devil, either way you are being used to push the agenda of a kingdom. Jesus does not believe in keeping people around you who is not helping you advance a course. He believes that those who are not helping you to build is actually destroying what you are building. Anyone in a team who is not advancing the interest of the team is actually destroying the team. There is nobody who will say I will just be there and do nothing that should be allowed to be there in the first place. Why? Because if they are not doing anything they are sowing the seed of discouragement and weakness on others who should be doing something. Sometimes they will talk and say see, I am tired of how things are being done there so I decided to seat and watch to see what becomes of the team. Immediately such is said no matter who it was said to, it will indirectly begin to affect their productivity energy and they will start to question if this thing is actually going towards the right direction. Before you know it he/she will have the talk with another person and within couple of days or weeks the team is polluted and things begins to fall apart. On no account should you allow anybody who is not totally committed to your course to stay on your team or else he or she will destroy the entire team. *If you are willing to die for something then you must surround yourself with people who will be willing to die for that thing.* The reason the gospel continued after Jesus had gone to heaven was because those, he committed the gospel to their hands was totally sold out to the gospel and were willing to die for it. Thomas said let us go also that we may die with him. Whenever one person admits to being tired in a project, suddenly everyone's energy begins to deflect. That is why you must be conscious of the people you choose to fight alongside with you in a battlefield. You need an Aaron and Hur if you must win in the battles of life. *"Exodus 17:11-12, and so it was, when Moses held up his hand, that Israel prevailed; and when he let down his hand, Amalek prevailed. But Moses hands became heavy so they took a stone and put it under him and he sat on it. And Aaron and Hur supported his hands one on one side and the other on the other side and his hands were steady until the going down of the sun".* God has already promised us victory but we cannot obtain that victory if we are not willing to fight for it. The bible is filled with stories of war that the preferred people of God had to fight. God gave the Israelites the city and asked them to go in and take it. You would think that once the Lord has commanded that you should go in and possess the land that the residue of the land will cooperate with you and allow you to take it without a fight. If that is what you believe then you have been taught wrong. David was anointed to be a king at the age of 17 and had to fight in many battles till he was 30 years old before he ascended the throne. Those battles were the thing that legitimized his anointing. What legitimizes your right to a position is what you are willing to fight in order to occupy that position. Sometimes you are left frustrated, in fact all you want to do is to serve the Lord. Maybe in a church you may choose to serve God in one capacity or the other but people in that team may make things difficult for you. Sometimes you wonder why you will say one thing and it is received as another thing. Nothing you do seem to be right. Yet all you want to do is to help in church and serve the Lord because you love the Lord and you expect people to see that what you really want to do is to serve. Of course, God knows that all you want to do is to serve Him but He would have to vet you before He can allow you to serve Him. He would want to know what you are willing to put up with because of Him. He cannot know the depth of your love for Him if you are not hurt multiple times yet stayed serving.

1Corinthians 3:13, each one's work will become clear; for the day will declare it, because it will be revealed by fire; and the fire will test each one's work, of what sort it is.

Look if you are a person who easily gets offended, the Lord will not do much with you, and the will of God for us is that we bear much fruit not just fruit but much fruits and that our fruits should remain. *To bear fruit is one thing to keep the fruit is another.* You may through charisma gather crowd but you need character to keep them and true character is developed through experiences, hurts, betrayal and disappointments. Anything that hurts you so much was allowed by God to help build you up into the fullness of him. God wants people who will go through what he went through and still loves. So, when God wants to use you, he will kill emotional side of you that might affect the work negatively. And no matter how long it takes he will get it done, but whether it takes long or less will depend on our willingness to let go of ourselves and let him step in and prep us for his usage.

If he could go to the cross because of you, couldn't you endure a little hardship because of him? Every born-again believer is a potential captain that could be used to destroy the troops of darkness, but it will all depend on the kind of training he/she will be willing to allow himself/herself to be subjected to. *Whenever we think ourselves to be strong, a little storm will rise to find out how strong we really are.* I have seen people who use everything within their power to try and stop stories against them. Some will pay the media houses just to cover up blackmailing stories against them meanwhile in such cases GOD wanted to use such stories to elevate them. I have seen people who go through difficult persecution that many people believe there is definitely no coming back from that, actually comes out stronger and even leads to their global launching. The ways of God are totally different from the ways of man. Whenever God would allow His children to go through difficult times, he has something of consolation value for them. Everyone is born with a destiny and every destiny has a path. Every path has potholes, stumbling blocks and mountains. You must submit yourself to undergo the discipline that makes for your destiny. The bible is constantly reminding us of an impending persecution. If we continue in bread-and-butter Christianity, are you sure any of us can survive when the prophesied persecution comes? 'Williams Tyndale' was strangled and burned to dead at stake in the year **'1536'** for translating the bible into English. There are many like him who paid with their lives for the sake of the gospel. *The gospel came to us on the altar of sacrifice.* JESUS who is the center of the gospel was crucified, his followers were killed, some were behead, some were crucified and another boiled in a hot oil and later bound with stone and thrown into the sea, some were stoned to dead.

Those who started the gospel and some who continued with the pure gospel died for the sake of the gospel. That is still the reason why those who preaches the pure gospel of Christ today still faces persecution. If at some point you are having doubts if you are called or whether you are doing the right thing because of the multitude of what you are going through, confuse no more brother, worry no more sister, you are called and are also doing the right thing. *"And let us not be weary in well doing, for in due season we shall reap if we faint not. Galatians.6:9"*

CHAPTER SEVEN

Association Matters

I f you want to burn for God, you must join yourself with people who are burning for God. In this kingdom everything is done intentionally. Friendship must be vetted through the Holy Spirit, Association must be decided for you by the spirit. ***"Proverbs 27:17, as iron sharpens iron, so one person sharpens another".***

You need someone who will push you to pray, you need someone who can discipline you and hold you accountable if you stray from the truth. You must subject yourself to be corrected no matter how gifted you are. Those who only clap for you, is there to drain you but those who rebuke, correct and sometimes criticize you are there to sharpen you and make you a better soldier. If you desire to go far in life then allow somebody to question your revelation without you getting offended and you must have the patience to explain your stand to him if he doesn't understand you. Jesus will always explain to His disciples the things they did not understand. Contemporaries are good but a mentor is very necessary. A mentor is a person who can caution you and tell you where you are getting it wrong and you must humbly obey without argument. Every great man has someone counseling him almost all the time. Whenever you leave the vetting of your performance to contemporaries, you are on your way out of relevance. *If we want the Lord to do much with us then the ministry of submission and praying must never be outgrown.* Whatever you dream of doing someone else had already done it, it might not be exactly but similar. God arranged this race to be about submission and performance. He wants us to be connected to one another and we are strongest when we are together.

CHAPTER EIGHT

Do A Follow Up

T his kingdom is about battles and anyone that comes into the fold, a proper follow up must accompany them. If it's a lady, it is advised that a sister who is well grounded should always check up on her and pray with her. And if it's a man a brother that is also strong in faith should do a follow up with him and also pray with him. Why should you choose the gender that should do a follow up? Because nobody is above temptation. The devil is constantly looking for ways to bring down anyone that is seen as a weapon against his agenda in the world. Even old and new members should not be left out. The devil is always going around planting ideas in the head of the people, planting faults in their minds against the church of the living God. Some brethren might stop going to church because in a whole month nobody called to check on them and that could stir up offense in their hearts and the devil will have occasion to enter their life to mess things up. Since we are in a war against the kingdom of darkness be aware that some people might not want to listen to you when you are trying to get them to be in the lord. Some, offense will be so heavy in their hearts but you must use the weapon of consistency, gentleness and spiritual tenacity to get them back into the house of God. *On no account should we get offended when offended people are making it difficult for us to get them back into the church.* What you must understand is that the devil might not have a problem with a person going to church but his only problem will be, whenever the person begins to attend the church that has the capacity of changing their lives and delivering them out of his claws, he will begin to devise all kinds of means to try and keep them out of that church. But those that are not ignorant of his devises will fight tooth and nail with him till a child of GOD is rescued from his control. God always leaves the 99 to go after the one that is missing. We are constantly being pulled on every side. On the other side God is pulling us to himself and on the other side the devil is trying to pull us to himself. As a soldier in the lord's army, you must resist him at all time and teach others never to pay him attention and resist him always. *"Proverbs 27:23, Be thou diligent to know the state of thy flocks, and look well to thy herds".*

CHAPTER NINE

O n the altar of prayer every matter is addressed, God gave us the concept of prayer so that we through it can access anything we may need in life. God desperately wants to give us the things we want but he cannot come down to our level, we must ascend up to his level in order for us to access the things we want. The idea is to make man take up the form of God and have rule over the earth and even over the affairs of the spirit. We are made in the image of God and His likeness but the only way we can truly manifest the fullness of God is in our engagement in the place of prayer. Strength in the kingdom is developed in the place of prayer, higher spiritual capacity is developed in the place of prayer. *A prayerless Christian cannot enjoy the fullness of God's power and we need power if we must have dominion.* Jesus Christ himself often withdrew into the wilderness and prayed, *Luke 15:16*. No amount of prayer is too much prayer and as long as the earth remains prayer cannot be considered old-school. Prayer is still the only way to obtain power from the power house of God. When the apostles ran into trouble for preaching the resurrection from the dead, they prayed.

Acts 4:23-31: 'On their release, Peter and John went back to their own people and reported all that the chief priests and the elders had said to them. When they heard this, they raised their voices together in prayer to God. "Sovereign Lord," they said, "you made the heavens and the earth and the sea, and everything in them. You spoke by the Holy Spirit through the mouth of your servant, our father David:

"Why do the nations rage

and the peoples plot in vain?
The kings of the earth rise up
and the rulers band together
against the Lord and against his anointed one"

Indeed Herod and Pontius Pilate met together with the Gentiles and the people of Israel in this city to conspire against your holy servant Jesus, whom you anointed. They did what your power and will had decided beforehand should happen. Now, Lord, consider their threats and enable your servants to speak your word with great boldness. Stretch out your hand to heal and perform signs and wonders through the name of your holy servant Jesus. "After they prayed, the place where they were meeting was shaken. And they were all filled with the Holy Spirit and spoke the word of God boldly.

Prayer is the channel made available to us the children of God if we truly want to have access to those things created for our benefits. Prayer brings you up to certain spiritual frequency where you can have access to the things you may have need of. Prayer gives you access to the father and he desperately wants to hear your voice and nothing is considered too much for you to ask. You can literally ask for anything you need no matter how big. Imagine walking into a bank knowing that any amount of money you sign for will be given to you, how much will you sign for? *Prayer puts you in a position where nothing can be denied you when you ask in faith.* So, as a soldier in the Lord's army prayer is what arms you with all the spiritual weapons you need and no amount of prayer is too much prayer. The prayers that seem not to be answered will be answered in your children. So, pray and keep praying no prayer falls to the ground. Whenever you have chance to attend prayer meetings please do. Never you get tired of praying for some prayers made today will bring answers tomorrow. If you know that all your prayers get answered how many times will you pray? And how much prayer is enough prayer? Actually, no prayer is enough prayer. Prayer gives you access into the deciding court of heaven. When we pray, we are settling matters in the spirit and are sometimes in the court room of heaven correcting and reversing negative verdict that has been passed against you and your family or even against others. Anyone that must be an effective soldier in Christ must pray constantly and consistently. 'Prayer is the master key'.

IN CONCLUSION

"2 Timothy 2:21,
If a man therefore purge himself from these, he shall be a vessel unto honour, sanctified, and meet for the master's use, and prepared unto every good work".

Get ready! Get ready! Get ready!

Burn down any bridge that will take you back to the place of shame and dishonor. Disconnect yourself from programs that pollutes your spirit. Intentionally remove yourself from associations that crumbles your spiritual stability. Avail yourself for the Master's use and dedicate yourself to Him. Eat things permitted by the spirit only not by men. Go to places allowed by your anointing not by men. Do things that brings the master glory. Go into the kingdom of darkness in the place of prayer and rescued captured men and captured destinies in the prison holds of the devil. God wants to use you, prepare yourself. Purge yourself, rid yourself of besetting sins, and separate yourself from anything that will entangle you into pleasing the flesh. Set yourself on Holy Ghost fire let the fire of revival start through you and burn off the impurities around your life. Higher ground await you therefore purge yourself. You can ascend higher than this, there is still more for you. See you on the other side of fire.

www.ingramcontent.com/pod-product-compliance
Lightning Source LLC
Chambersburg PA
CBHW051001030426
42339CB00007B/430